The End and

After

How to survive when the ash settles

Contents

The Overall Situation

The Doomsday Disaster

We live in a nice and cozy society. High caloric food is available at our fingertips, information at the touch of a button, and we can work without breaking a sweat. We can travel in hours a distance that took our ancestors months to traverse.   We can pick up a small electronic device and instantly communicate to anyone in the world If we need to get in contact with someone. It doesn't take months for us to get news from any place in the world. We have everything we want available now. We stand on a pedestal of luxury.

The higher we get the more we will fall when our cozy cushion we call society crumbles beneath our feet.

We don't know how it will happen, but it is only a matter of time until it does. The earth and its people are not stable. It only takes a little push to unbalance the whole stacked system enough for it to no longer stands. I have no idea how we have made it so long without this already happening.

There are many different situations that can cause a global societal collapse. Since this is a survival guide, I'm not going to cover anything that will eradicate the entire population (i.e. the sun exploding, complete destruction of the atmosphere, nanobots eating everything carbon based, a meteor the size of the moon hitting earth, etc.). For a few of us to survive, the situation needs to be survivable.

No matter the crisis, people will return home to protect their families. Looting will become a common practice and murder a frequent occurrence. Some people will flee or isolate themselves while others will band together to protect each other. Multiple mass migrations will occur as people use up the resources around them and are forced to flee to another area. Everyone who lives through doomsday will have one goal in mind: survive.

Those who survive a doomsday event do so because of one reason: luck. It doesn't matter what supplies you have, where and what you live in, or how much training you have put yourself through, if an apocalyptic meteor falls on your head, you are not going to survive. This book may not help you survive the day of doom, but hopefully the day after.

This book was created to help increase your chances of post-apocalyptic survival. It will help you know what to expect, create a plan of action, and stockpile the necessary equipment to survive. The more prepared you are, the better the chance you give yourself of living through the aftermath of the worst disasters earth can ever experience.

It's not like a doomsday scenario has a high chance of occurring. These types of events are rare. But they can happen. It only takes one apocalyptic event to cause countries to collapse. What follows is a list of possible events that could spell out destruction to the life we know. It is by no means a complete list of doomsday scenarios. The future can be full of surprises. As much as we try to expect the unexpected, expect not to expect everything.

Each of the following situations could happen alone and cause global devastation, but it is more likely that one would cause another to occur, and the dominoes of destruction will destroy life as we know it.

Multiple Massive Earthquakes

The earth's crust is a crowded mass of floating islands playing bumper cars with each other. When one pushes, it is felt across the others. One huge earthquake can set off others echoing across the world and terrible aftershocks repeatedly rumbling the rubble. Major roadways will be destroyed, bridges collapsed, buildings crumbled, damns cracked and spilling. Gas and electrical pipelines will rupture causing multiple fires. Water pipelines will burst, spilling out and wasting that precious resource. Nothing can destroy an area like an earthquake.

Nothing will impede help from arriving like an earthquake. Roadways and runways will be destroyed or blocked. Buildings will be unsafe for rescuers to enter because of the risk of a gas line exploding or the entire structure coming down. Help will be needed everywhere and assistance available to only a few. In most major earthquakes many of the casualties occurred because help was too late getting there. Imagine multiple major earthquakes happening within a few days of each other.

Beyond the devastation around the epicenter, the earthquakes can cause tsunamis that will devastate coastal cities across the world. Even places that don't feel the shaking will wash away in the waves.

Cities collapsing, burning, or flooding. Help cut off. Death under every stone. The power of earthquakes can easily crack and crumble the foundation of our lives.

Historical Precedence:

- San Francisco earthquake (1906)
  - The fire alone flattened half of the city. This earthquake injured over half the population of the San Francisco. This hasn't even been close to the worst earthquake in history. There have been other earthquakes that have killed nearly a million people from a few second shake.

Meteor Shower

A house sized rock coming to earth can destroy half a city. A city sized rock can destroy most of the life on the planet. A rock the size of a state would obliterate all life. A rock the size of a country could shatter the earth like a ball of ice. We won't deal with anything larger than a city, because we wouldn't be alive long to deal with it. Falling rocks are one of the few disasters that can literally destroy the planet, not just the fragile life scratching the surface.

Not only could these falling rocks from the sky cause explosions greater than any nuclear bomb, but they can also trigger the symptoms of earthquakes mentioned before and cause other demographic destroyers. A huge meteor can punch a hole through our protective ozone layer, create fire storms the size of hurricanes, earthquakes shaking the earth like a battered water balloon, tsunamis that march uphill miles past the coastline, and explosions that make the nuclear bomb look like a firecracker. All are fatal ingredients that make the recipe of disaster cooked by a rock from space.

Historical Precedence:

- Dinosaur extinction.
    - This is the one real time when earth faced a doomsday scenario. If this rock was any bigger, we might not be alive to call earth home. This one rock nearly wiped-out life on earth. 70% of life was destroyed, including the greatest animals ever to tread this fertile planet. The greater the species the greater they fall. We are standing dominant on the top now. A meteor caused a mass extinction before, it can easily happen again.

Massive Volcanic Eruption

This is just like large meteor striking the earth, without the intervention of a space rock. What makes a large eruption worse is the amount of debris that a volcano throws into the air. This massive mound can spew more pollution than mankind has ever put into the air. Global warming or a volcanic winter may both occur. Toxic gas and volcanic ash can kill more than the rock and lava it spits out.

Those are just the short-term effects. Unlike the dust from a bomb, a volcanic cloud may take years to descend. Without that precious sunlight, crops will fail. Without plants, animals are next, including us. A massive eruption can wipe most of our food supply. What the volcano doesn't directly kill, starvation may take care of.

Historical precedence:

- Pompeii.
    - A perfect example of the immediate destructive power of a volcano that destroyed a civilization.

- Yellowstone massive eruption.
    - This is one example of the power of a huge eruption. The ash cloud created by this prehistoric eruption covered most of the United States. If this happened today, the U.S. of A. will be destroyed. Its people, its government, its power and influence all buried under a heavy layer of ash.

- The ice age
    - It's theorized that a massive eruption is what caused the ice age. This event killed off 90% of the human population. Imagine the billions who would die today if an event like this happened again.

Government Collapse of a Super Power

The world is so globally united, if one major link in the chain breaks, this could collapse the entire global system. Governments are making, buying, selling, and loaning to each other. Many of these transactions are keeping countries functioning. A superpower collapsing would cause a domino effect, and other countries will follow. Other superpowers may be able to survive for a little, but with no resources coming in they won't be able to stand for long.

Historical Precedence:

- Hurricane Katrina.
    - In the wake of the damns breaking the social structure was swept away as the flood waters came in. People turned on their neighbors and even shot at rescuers.

- Stock market crashing.
    - This happened in the United States, but it plunged the entire world into the Great Depression. Without the help and support of an organization for the people, many perished from everything from starvation to suicide. The Jobless rate of the Great Depression can easily happen (and has happened) in an always fragile economy.

War

Even a small war within a country could cause complete destruction to the framework of society. The opposing sides would be evenly matched which leaves little left in the country after the destruction. These are not some rebels out for anarchy, this is a country torn in half. Even if it is a civil war of a world power, this could easily cause a government collapse previously mentioned. The floods of a local war could easily spread and sweep other countries into the current as the two sides reach out for assistance. Suddenly a world war kills countries under the tides of war.

Historical precedence:

- World War 1: Something as little as one person dying set off a fire of war that engulfed the entire world. Wars have a terrible habit of pulling everyone else in.   Because of the death and destruction of this war it was known as the "war to end all wars." Even though the trenches filled with blood, WWI wasn't the worst, it was only the first.

Near Extinction of a Global Resource

All the other events happen in an instant, but loosing food, water, oil, etc. will be a slow and painful demise. There are many factors that can cause a resource to fail. Oil reserves can dry up. Abnormal weather, volcanic ash, or nuclear fallout can contaminate and destroy crops and water. Plants can get sick too so a pandemic of wheat, corn, or any other important produce could cause cascading catastrophes.

As the demand for said resources increases, so will the world unrest. This may lead to war as countries strive to find these resources in someone else's land. We need the substance to live our normal lives, and we will spend what it takes to live. So as the resource rises in price, the people will pay. Sadly, people will start trading essential survival gear for a mouthful of food. Starvation will strike even harder when people have nothing left to sell. The economy of the world will drop and shatter on the floor of chaos.

Oil is the most probable scenario. It is not reusable like food or water; we are on our way to running out of our limited supply. Of all the dooms day scenarios, this one is most likely to occur. Our cars are taking us down a one-way road to devastation.

Historical precedence:

- Famine and food restrictions in Africa. Food shortage has started wars. Crowds of hungry hoards have had bullets spray through them in their attempt to get a commodity so precious they were willing to risk their lives to obtain and so valuable their government couldn't give it up.

- Venezuela economic collapse 2016. Because of inflation the price to produce food fell below the price to sell food. Stores were not able to afford food, and neither could the people. So they looted and cleared what was left on the shelves. This caused the entire country to destabilize.

Technology Failing

Another resource that we depend heavily on is technology. Cell phones, computers, and television all allow us to communicate and connect to the world. What if they were to suddenly stop sending and receiving? It can be some mega computer virus, an electromagnetic pulse (EMP), global power outage, solar flare hitting the earth, or something else that permanently flips the off switch.

An EMP is a powerful pulse released during a nuclear explosion and destroys electronic equipment. But EMP specific bombs can explode without a nuclear mushroom cloud. This causes more than just computers crashing or circuit boxes flipping. Cars will die where they roll, phones will fail; computers: flat line. Anything caught in the blast zone of an EMP will be instantly thrown into the dark ages. Communication will be instantly lost with the world. An electrical failure affects us more than our ability to check emails and updates. Security alarms will fail, electrical heating and air conditioning will freeze, and hospital machines will lose their lives. Imagine the deaths that will occur in a hospital if all electricity-sucking systems stop (an EMP will also destroy back-up generators). If a power outage happens in the winter imagine the thousands that may freeze before heat can be found.

A technological crash could quite easily send a city into chaos. Imagine if multiple EMP bombs where set off in large key cities. We depend so much on electronic technology; it failing could easily cause a crash that sends cracks that collapse the economic world.

Historical Precedence

- New York Black Out
  - One of the worst blackouts experienced in the United States. Block after block blacked out and were burglarized. 500 police officer were injured in the attempt to quench the quell, and nearly 5000 civilians were also hurt. I'm sure most weren't career criminals, but jumping back to the Stone Age can turn people into cavemen.

- Y2K scare.
  - Many can remember the panic a simple count created. It's hard to believe that a computer not knowing how to count to a couple thousand could spell out doom to the world society. Planes falling from the sky, buildings shutting down, computers exploding. There were many synopses that theorist thought would play out. Luckily all the doomsday theories proved false... for that event. A virus or something similar

could cause a similar situation to actually come true.

Pandemic

Pandemic: A disease with a high fatality rate and extremely contagious. With the speed of global transportation, a disease like this could spread faster than we can track it. The Spanish influenza, bird flu, swine flu, or most of all the other popularized "pandemics" haven't even been close to a real-world threat. There could be a worse disease just waiting to be passed onto humanity. Imagine something that can kill half the population. That's like wiping out everyone in Asia.

The wave of disease will spread like ripples in a pond, but things will settle as the virus dies out. Diseases need human hosts to survive. They can't survive a sunny day or freezing winter outside of the human body. A virus will die out so that it can't find anymore new hosts to make a home in. Those who survive the pandemic will either be immune or were able to isolate themselves enough to not get the virus. If this virus has no immunity, there will be very few survivors left after the virus burns away. Society would be but be gone by the time the survivors climb out of their bubbles and camps.

Historical Precedence:

- Black plague
    - The black plague of the medieval times has been the most volatile of viruses, killing a fourth of the known world's population. That would be like the population of the Americas –north, central, and south – and Europe getting wiped out today. The black plague spread without fast global transportation we have today that passes diseases around.

Nuclear holocaust

This is not just one nuclear explosion in a populated area; this is attack and counterattack with nuclear weapons. Large cities will be destroyed, capitals in ruins, and fallout spreading forth on the four winds. Nuclear ash will descend and poison crops, water supplies and people.

A nuclear holocaust is likely to happen as a result of a world war. As the sides continue to fight to a stale mate, countries will become more desperate. In search for a solution we will remember the past. It was a nuclear bomb that ended World War II; it could end another world war, right? That only works when one side has the fire power. Nuclear attack and counterattack would end the war, but little survivors would be able to tell about it.

Historical precedence

- Hiroshima.
    - It is argued that the only reason Japan surrendered was because they realized the nuclear bombs could completely decimate the entire country. Every man, woman and child would be melted away in a nuclear wave if they didn't give up the fight. Will we remember that lesson of eradication or settle pressing the buttons of retribution?

A Super Drug

Drug technology and potency have recently increased dramatically. It is only a matter of time before a cure for a disease, a performance enhancer given to soldiers or athletes, or an illegal drug is created that sends society sliding down into an addictive haze. A doomsday drug may either have little effect on or even increases body function.

Something like this is necessary for the drug to cover the population in addictive smoke. If it was destroying the economy, it would be regulated like any other illegal drug. But if it shows that it can be beneficial in moderation, why would the government stop something that improves the people?

The enhancement alone may be enough to leave the user extremely addicted, but there are likely other chemicals that create a dependency. When first addicted the drug may initially be used to improve work, performance, or recovery. But as dependence slowly increases their productivity will decrease. Work, family, friends will lose importance as the drug becomes their entire life.

Like any drug, there is always a risk of an overdose. Even though the drug could provide some benefit, in the end it destroys the person. Before death, the person is likely to lose their job. Without income, they will be forced to borrow, lie, steal, and kill to get to their drug.

Those who overdose may be a small number at first, but this number could steadily rise until most of the population is addicted. Addicted government official might argue that the drug is a commodity and influences the government to go to war to obtain it from the countries that have more of it. Then the drug becomes a ration to improve the soldier's performance which increases the addiction even more.

By the end, society will become so addicted to the substance they won't know how to get off of it. Regulating the drug will become impossible as law makers, enforcers, and abiding citizens are all on the drug. Overdosing will increase as the potency is augmented, less work will be done, and society will come to a screeching halt.

A sign of the times is the legalization of marijuana. Weed can cause the downfall of society? Yes, it is possible. Everything that has been described about a doomsday drug describes the characteristics of marijuana. Weed does affect someone's work ethic, criminal thinking, and motivation, but doesn't damage the body like other drugs and it doesn't impair a person as much either...today.

Marijuana potency has increased by 160% in the last twenty years, and it is still rising. We don't know when weed will reach dangerous levels, but if (or when) it does and it is legal everywhere, it may be too late to stop the addiction.

Weed may turn into what cocaine is now. Cocaine didn't have the addictive qualities when it was first used. It was considered safe and was even put in sodas that kids drank. Cocaine use to be a mild medicinal plant that didn't cause a great addiction and had little risk of overdose.

But that has changed now. Cocaine has been cooked and cut and is now one of the most addictive drugs today. It is now a killer. Marijuana might be heading down the same path.

Historical Precedence:

- Powerful dynasties in China fell because of opium drug addiction.
  - A drug collapsed country. In China, the country fell into addiction starting a war they lost. This is the reason Hong Kong was lost to China. After this war settled with unequal treaties, China entered into a "Century of humiliation."

- Cigarettes and lung cancer.
  - Before it was discovered that cigarettes kill, nearly half of the population smoked. Today it is still one of the biggest killers. Imagine if this was something more addicting.

- The addiction of morphine given to soldiers during WWII.
  - Morphine was a drug that helped the injured soldiers on the battlefield, but they came back as drug addicts.

- Drugs given to soldiers in warring countries in Africa and Afghanistan.
    - To help ease fear and relieve pain, generals would give their soldiers drugs. Their soldiers became so dependent on the drug that it became their paycheck. If they survived their term they remained lifelong addicts, doing anything for the drug.

It is just gangs; what problem can they cause? Of all the possible scenarios listed in this book, this one has caused most of the collapses in history.

Gangs are generally criminal in nature. They function outside the law. They are well armed and well organized in ways that are difficult to track. They have an efficient way to recruit and install a life-long loyalty.

Gang members are from the streets and would be the first to take to the streets when problems arise. These problems could be a major economic setback, religious or racial issues, or political squabble. Whatever the motive, the spark doesn't have to be that big to unite gangs in common cause.

Police forces will try to quench the flames of violence, but it will be like bringing a garden hose to a forest fire. It will be an unprepared reactionary force and taken by surprise. With law enforcement not sufficient, those not in a gang will be forced to take force against the gang to defend their family or territory. This will force law enforcement to attack regular citizens who felt forced to attack the gangs.

This will start a triangle war: law enforcement, unified gangs, and defending citizens all attacking each other. Of course each of these branches will call for reinforcements. When one gets more power the other will request more help to equalize. The violence will continue to escalate until something collapses. This could be the incident that causes a collapse of a power or escalate a civil war to a world war.

This war could escalate quicker if the population sides with the organized criminal element. The Revolutionary War was started like this. The population sided with a rebel cause which provided the rebels with reinforcement and support. This defeated the strongest empire of the time.

Criminal organizations can also be called rebels or terrorists. And these groups have been powerful enough to topple governments and outmatch militaries.

Historical Precedence

- Egyptian Government collapse
    - Rebels had enough power to collapse the government more than once.

- Afghan War
    - Gangs united under a religious pretext forced a war that lasted a decade.

- Libya Civil War
    - A group of rebels were powerful enough to force the country into a bloody stand still and dethrone its government leaders.

SIDE NOTE: The Reality of a Zombie Pandemic

I'm definitely not saying the corpses and cadavers coming alive and crawling out of their graves to feed on living brains is a possible apocalyptic scenario.   An alien invasion is more likely to happen. But there are some situations that can cause society to fall into a zombie-like state.

You can call a zombie apocalypse a pandemic. There is a possibility that a disease or drug may be made, altered, or already exists that doesn't necessarily kill its victim, but drives them mad. No it won't stop the heart -- we kind of need that to function -- but it could primitize the brain. People who have gone mad have been known to eat other people. A drug or disease could cause this insanity.

It doesn't have to be a chemical that creates zombie-like hoards. During a disaster the general population is going to change. Normal law-abiding citizens will become criminals. Those who would never dream of robbery, rape, or murder will become robbers, rapists, and murderers during and after a world disaster. Mobs of desperate citizens will roam the streets in search for supplements. People will be murdered by these mobs. What the general public might do in an apocalyptic scenario could be very similar to a zombie revolution.

Desperation changes everything. When starving, human meat has become an enticing treat. When dying of thirst, blood becomes a deluded drink. When pushed to his limits, man can lose all sense of civility; and a zombie-like creature can rise in his place.

Historical precedence:

- Rabies.
  - Here is a virus that is spread by the bite that causes the victim to become aggressive and lose a normal state of mind. Sounds like the perfect precursor to zombies.

- L.A. Riots
  - People running the streets destroying anything in their path. Random acts of violence left dozens of dead and billions of dollars in damage. Crowds gone crazy that required armies to restore the peace.

- PCP
  - PCP is a hallucinogenic drug that has caused zombie like symptoms in those who abused it; including eating people.

SIDE NOTE: Alien invasion not included

I know a meteor shower or food disappearing from the planet are not likely to happen, but those *could* happen, *and* mankind has a possibility of surviving. I am not including a common doomsday theory of an alien invasion because the situation needs to be survivable. Any extraterrestrial race that has the technology to travel thousands of light-years to this planet will have the technology to destroy the indigenous population without us putting up a fight.

If I was an alien overlord with my greedy over-sized green eyes set on settling a new world for my galactic queen insect, I would definitely not waste resources and exoskeleton armored soldiers on an invasion. An interplanetary conquest does not fall under the rules of the Geneva Convention. And aliens aren't stupid.

So, if I was a general out to get rid of humans, I would launch simpler and more efficient methods of destruction. With an advanced technology at my suction-cup fingertips, introducing a genetically engineered virus specifically designed to eradicate the biggest threat on earth –humans – would be easily in my technologically-advanced arsenal. Package it in a small unnoticed meteorite. Send that to earth and sit back and watch from the stars as the human population tries in vain to find a cure. Humans can barely fight earth viruses; imagine the trouble with an advanced alien one.

Watching safely behind the moon as my virus does its destructive job, I wait until mankind hangs on by a thread. But I still won't send down my six-legged soldiers. I got lasers! Or some other type of deadly distance weapon. With those weapons at my disposal, it'll be easy enough to cut down those last pockets of people persistently populating the planet.

No one would survive, no one could hide. Human satellites can read a newspaper on a clear day; imagine what alien technology will be able to see from the stars. Any person left will be able to be picked off from space. By the time the actual invasion starts, there will be no one left to stand up to them. Earth would be an unprotected paradise just perfect for my alien colony.

That situation could occur if the aliens actually wanted the resources we have. If for some reason we just pissed them off and they wanted to destroy all life, they still don't need any invasion or "Death Star" gun. Knocking some large rocks off course of the asteroid belt would do the trick and it wouldn't cost them any resources.

Movies depict mankind putting up a valiant fight against the disc-flying destroyers. But in reality (kind of) their advanced technology could destroy us without us being able to fire any of our weapons. The conflict would be like a man with a spear fighting a stealth bomber. We would likely be dead before we ever saw it coming. No one would be able to escape or survive an alien genocide. So let's just hope that never happens!

Historical Precedence:

None that could be verified. If something like this happened before, we wouldn't be here now.

Situation specifics

There are many different situations that can spell out doom to the multitudes. In each circumstance there are also many different aspects that will be affected, here are a few:

Media

In the initial stages, news of the cataclysm will be over every media source. We may even get extended coverage if we are not at ground zero. But as power outages increase, the media reports will die down. One of the first things that will go is internet and phone services. Phones will soon die and remain dead as they become overloaded with everyone trying to phone friends and family to make sure they are ok. With phones failing, soon the internet will follow. Cable television will then black out, and later satellite. Local public transmission will remain on emergency broadcast channels, but with no revenue coming in, reporters will have little reason to work, and soon there will be nothing to broadcast. Radio stations may last the longest as they can be run by a single person. As radio stations are raided, destroyed, or abandoned because of power outages, the only reliable form of communication will be two-way and Hamm radios... Until those batteries run dry.

Populated Areas

Large cities will become mini warzones as rival groups compete for resources. Some specific danger areas include:

- Stores
  - Not just grocery stores, even though they would be hit the hardest. With 911 not answering, people will think it is payday and will raid any store to get rich quick. It is not always about getting supplies. Having expensive items to trade for goods may be just as good. But how much will a big screen TV be worth with no power to run it?

- Wealthy neighborhoods
  - If you need something that others have, who is most likely to have it? The rich. They can afford food storage and supplies. They have fancy treasures for trading. Security is also limited in looters heads, even if the rich

can afford an armada. Because even if they have weapons, the personnel are likely to be limited and less than a mob or gang. Like shops in a riot, wealthy areas will draw crowds of desperate people.

- Places along the freeway
  - The interstate links the country. Even if the freeway is blocked by abandoned cars, groups will walk along the freeway when they move to different locations. Just like how we stop for food and gas when we go on a road trip, so will they. But they won't have any interest in leaving a resource behind or paying for what they need if money is worthless. They take out and take off.

Large cities will be cutthroat with first skirmishes for supplies, and then battles as groups try to raid other groups. Smaller cities will be cut off from help, or abandoned as resources are pooled to bigger population centers. The only people coming to visit will either be in desperation or deception. Small towns will build up walls to protect their small society. They will be more stable than other places and protect the piece of peace they have. Because of limited supplies in a small town, they will likely turn away individual families seeking help.

A small town may feel like a safe haven for those who are in that society, but desperation will lead to escalation, and the need for resources may bind a group together large enough to attack and overcome the small city's defenses.

Even small towns don't have limitless supplies. As their supplies run low, they may begin to raid and then rage war on neighboring towns. Towns may bind together, or towns may later destroy each other. These alliances and battles may be the start of a vicious gun toting society.

The Population

When the world crisis occurs, the general population is going to panic. There will be a rush toward stores as people either try to get the supplies they think they will need to survive, or try and get rich quick. As people fight each other over diminishing supplies, they resort to murder. A guy with a gun is likely to get away with a lot of loot... until he meets another guy with a gun out for supplies or vengeance.

Populations may be divided between those who stay and those who move. Multiple mass exoduses may occur as people hear the promise of a safe, supplied, sanctuary. But it is not likely to be peaceful populations of pilgrims. If they are leaving homes on some notion of a promised land, they obviously are not living any better at home. Supplies are likely to be short and people aren't likely to be taking enough supplies to make it all the way to their destination. These groups of people are going to be looting on their way.

Those already prepared or too timid to try and take treasures will hunker in home. Many will believe that the crisis wasn't as bad as the media says it is and will think that they can wait it out. The average family does have a month's supply of food in their pantries and refrigerator (if properly rationed) but will soon run out of water.

The majority of the population turning to theft will be too much for any police force to control. Where would you call the National Guard when there is rioting everywhere? Local law enforcement may be able to maintain order in certain places, but with every convenient store and supermarket being raided, they will not be able to cover all places and will likely pick government offices to protect. Another probable target to be protected would be gun stores. Nothing could be worse than having a raging mob, becoming a well-armed angry mob.

The problem occurs when the mob is already well armed, and there are already groups of well-armed, less then lawful individuals. Gangs will also be looking to survive. They will come together to not only get supplies, but also get rich. Gangs look for power, and with a diminished and busy police force not in full power to suppress them, they can easily arm themselves with raids to even secured and protected locations.

It's gangs that would make city dwelling so dangerous. Well-armed and organized, they will not settle with raiding stores and companies, but they will send groups out to raid house to house; especially in their self-claimed territories which will expand as they grow stronger. As groups come together, the gangs will become stronger. There will be even more gangs, and they will be more powerful.

Transportation

No matter the crisis, major roadways will be unusable by car. A virus or a nuclear explosion will cause congestion and abandoned vehicles as people flee the infected zones. Earthquakes will damage roads and cause more dead ends with more abandoned vehicle roadblocks. With transportation impaired at a national level, the economy quickly and continually collapses as no trade in goods occurs.

Local roadways may still be accessible, but cars are gas guzzlers. The most fuel-efficient cars will last the longest with motorcycles and scooters being the last gas users on the road.

Alternative powered vehicles (electric, propane, etc.) will later rule the roadways. Sadly, they are not mass produced. Other forms of transportation would take over, specifically bicycles and other self-powered ways of transport. Horses will be seen on the streets again.

Air travel may continue for a little, but as airports become more congested, they will eventually fail. Small private planes may continue for as long as they have access to fuel, which wouldn't be very long. Gas is imported from around the world, with imports gone, so soon is refueling.

Fuel and other non-reusable resources

Gasoline will no longer be produced and transported. Gas stations will immediately raise prices to sell their last supplies, but within a few weeks all stations will be emptied. With the number of cars on the road, gas theft will become common. Gas tanks will be siphoned and drilled for their liquid gold. Soon lucrative people (possibly those who took over gas stations) will begin to stockpile this gas and sell it for goods (money is not likely to have much value) and will gain power as people become more desperate. The search for cars with fuel in them can become fatal.

Eventually as gasoline turns into a costly dangerous commodity to have, more and more people will switch to easy and practical alternatives. Horses will gain ground. Bicycles will weave through the dead cars on the roadways.

There will still be vehicles.   Gasoline cars can easily be converted into propane (subsidized by wood gas), and diesels can run off of biofuel for as long as fat drippings are saved. A few lucrative oil workers may return to their site and trade refined oil at a ridiculously high price. But places far from these refineries (like the majority of the population) won't have access to this luxury.

As each year passes without products being produced, the use of non-reusable resources will diminish. Even the best batteries won't last ten years. By then gasoline will be long burned up. Unless oil refinery and distribution somehow resume, a decade after a disaster will see a world reverted back to eighteenth century technology. Only reusable power sources (i.e. solar and wind) will have the continuous power to escape the digression in technology.

Government

Local and federal government will still try to continue to function, but with damage to transportation and limited resources to fly into places, the government will diminish to nearly nonexistence. As their funding is reduced, they will let go more and more people employed by them. With governments collapsing across the world, they may not see a need (or have the funding) for a large standing army (not to mention the soldiers may abandon their area to return and protect their family). Bases will close, and cuts will hack away at the military personnel. Not just military will be cut. Post office, road construction, city power, police and fire men; they all are paid by taxes that will not be returned from the government. Who would work if they aren't getting paid to risk their lives to do so?

The government will still try to maintain communication through emergency channels, but as more places lose power even that hold will fail. As more politicians leave to help their families, the government will continue to weaken until all that is left is a skeleton government that doesn't run much of anything. Pockets of fractioned governments may still exist in larger populated areas where the military power can be close to their family. External powers will be nearly non-existent. Military personnel will only travel abroad when they know their family at home is safe. In a post-apocalyptic case, no one is safe.

In places with no government to protect them, people will carry protection on them. There is precedence for this. Look at countries with little to no functioning police system. Everyone is carrying around their own protection. The Middle East is a great example. Another example is the Wild West. Medieval times everyone had a sword at their belt. After Armageddon people are likely to do the same thing. Arguments will be settled with bullets. Avoid arguing.

One of the biggest threats from a government collapse is the financial support they provide to millions of people. Currency may still be used after a doomsday disaster, but government paychecks will stop. Not only are those employed by the government at risk. Welfare, retirement, disability funds, and unemployment pay will cease. Anyone who is not self-sufficient and depends on the government is at serious risk of being abandoned with nothing. No money means no way of paying for supplies. No work means no ability to contribute to a community who can only help those who help them. The disabled and elderly may be the first to die in a government collapse.

Jobs

As people rush home to protect their family, they will abandon their jobs. Most business will fail in a very short time. Some retail business may last longer as they continue to provide goods for people, but as their supplies dwindle their business will fall. Some positions of power may still hold strong and take over as mini governments for their local area (i.e. local military and police forces).

With people dead or gone, no one would be around to maintain water, communication, and power sources; all of which will soon fail after the global crisis.

Though the general population will abandon their jobs, people may search for those with specific training. As family members become sick or injured, people will seek out the assistance of known doctors in the neighborhood. Many doctors may say the same thing "I got to take care of my family first." In this case other families will trade supplies for assistance. As specific needs are requested services would be traded for survival gear and some semblance of employment may return.

In organized groups, necessary jobs will be assigned for the benefit of the community (for of an example of this see Convey or community)

Jobs fields likely to partly survive	Job fields likely to fail
Healthcare	Entertainment
Military (Mercenaries)	Production
Agriculture	Formal education
Repair and maintenance	Construction
Organized crime	Government employment
	Transportation
	Technology

Food

Mass food production will come to a screeching halt. Farms may continue to produce food for a little, but with the workers who don't live there returning to their homes and there is no way of transporting the goods, the decay of the products will force the farms to reduce in size. Only enough crops would be produced to support those who live at or close to the ranch to trade for food.

In rural areas looting will become frequent as people try to stay alive. Fatal food fights will be common. As people try to hide food and store more than they can keep the cache of edible gold will spoil. The demand for water will skyrocket and food will become a precious commodity. Many will die of starvation in rural areas as the food supplies burn up.

Many people will flee to the forests and mountains when a disaster strikes. All hunters and outdoor enthusiast will quickly take to the trees to find food. But the forest isn't an unlimited resource. Entire herds of deer and other large game will be extinguished as hunters gun down food, like every day is open season. Small animals will be next. Furry forest creatures surrounding the city will be wiped out to satiate the appetite of a starving race. The longer the time, the further out the forests will be destroyed. As ammunition dwindles, hunters will turn on each other to get the supplies they need to get the food they need.

After enough human death the demand for food will diminish and the herds and animals will eventually return. For larger game this may take years, but smaller animals could be back in a year. Supplies of food will be spoiled or used by then. Those who wish to survive more than a couple of years will need to be able to produce food.

Death

Death is going to be a frequent visitor. The initial crisis is going to have the largest death toll. With a virus this initial affect may be the largest.

As with any societal disaster, robbing and rioting will bring multiple homicides. There will be a small calm as people have gathered what they feel they need and have gone into hiding. But then the next storm front will roll in as these supplies start to dwindle.

Being so long without laws, murders will increase. This will escalate as people become more desperate for life-saving necessities. This death hurricane will last the longest until enough lives have been lost to reduce the demand of supplies. As prepackaged supplies dwindle those who have access to reusable supplies are likely to be the only ones who have a chance of surviving. The long-term death rate will still remain hirer than before the earth-ending event as access to medical supplies and experts will become more difficult.

The solution

Yes, this is a survival guide, but I'm not going to recommend how to live in the wild with nothing but a pocketknife. We don't go camping with only a machete, we pack prepared. Carry the most necessities you can for a given situation, and not only will you increase your chance of living, but you'll live more comfortably.

Get your supplies now

If you wait until a crisis happens to get equipped, you are going shopping too late. People will be rushing to the stores like it was the night before Christmas. Don't get caught in the frenzy. Those who are frantic for supplies will break every law and commandment imaginable. The most crowded crowds will quickly be dispersed when the first shot is fired. But people will leave to only get their own guns.

Burglarizing with bullets will become a blood bath. Even if you make it through the chaotic crowds, you are not likely to get everything you need. Everything of value will be out the sliding doors with a few days and store shelves aren't going to be restocked in a crisis. Even if you get your grimy gloves on gear, you're not guaranteed to make it back out again and keep the loot or your life. People will attempt to take from cold fingers if they feel it will keep them alive. Crisis shopping would be one of the most dangerous things you could do. Buy your bootie before you hear the boom.

Some supplies are superbly storable. Most non-food items (matches, containers, weaponry, etc.) can last forever if water, dirt, and excessive temperatures don't get into it. Since these products don't decompose, they can't be grown either, so don't expect to plant a survival soap seed after an emergency. Stock up now.

Food and some other supplies have expiration dates. Some food can last upwards of twenty years if stored properly. Most of this is food made specifically for emergency storage. Other less permanent provisions need to be rotated to keep all the food fresh.

Keep in mind the stuff that is not likely to be easily available after a disaster. Hopefully food and water will be found no matter what time it is on the doomsday clock. But other supplies are going to be taken and consumed all too quickly after Armageddon strikes. Beyond easily edible items, medicine, multivitamins, batteries, and fuel will be quickly consumed in the aftermath. Get those supplies before the cost costs you your life.

Get into shape

When we say store food, we don't mean stuff your face like a winterizing squirrel. Fat may be stored energy, but constantly carrying calories in your arteries and midsection could kill you. During and after a crisis you are likely going to be required to outrun innumerable onslaughts, climb over obstacles, and push yourself in ways that will challenge seasoned super soldiers. Be physically ready or you won't survive through the gauntlet of a post-apocalyptic life.

Without a social framework to catch us, life is going to be the survival of the fittest. What chance are you giving yourself by continuously camping on the couch?

Practice

Decide on your plan and practice it. Then decide on a plan "B" and practice that. You may need to pick locks, shoot weapons, create fires, etc. You think it is difficult doing those things now? Imagine the difficulty added with the pressure because your life may depend on a perfect shot, picked lock, or heated spot. Practice prior to the pressure and your chances of succeeding increase.

Hopefully you are equipping yourself with survival essentials. It may be too late to learn how to put together a flashlight in the dark when the lights go out for the last time. Become familiar with this equipment. Use it before you need it to save your life.

Go outside, go camping, go boating, and take road trips. Practicing can be a vacation, but the skills you get as a skilled vacationer can turn into necessary survival skills when you need it most.

Stay alive

A worldwide disaster affects people differently depending on their direction and distance to Ground Zero. If you need to run, run (don't forget to grab your pre-prepared pack first). If you can lock up and bunker down, get into your bunker. Rules may be broken to survive, don't be afraid to break them to stay alive. If at all possible, stay out of and away from trouble, but if trouble tries to find you, do whatever it may take to make it to tomorrow.

Don't panic

Running blindly out the door the moment you hear a loud boom may only save your life for a day or two. Stop and think. Do you need to leave immediately, or do you need to lock up? What supplies do you need to keep close and ready? If you're traveling, where are you going to go? What can you take with you? What supplies need to be hidden/locked up? Are there any supplies or people you need to risk your life to find and protect? Make sure you know exactly what you need to do before you go running off. Relax, breathe, and think. Processing through your situation will help keep you from panicking.

Get what you need and get safe

Hopefully the supplies you need are already in a room or basement, but few are going to be waiting at home for the clock to strike midnight. If your family is home and all together, great! If not, you are going to have to get them safe. This is risky but may be needed. Your family is always worth risking your life for. Supplies you are lacking may seem like they are nearly that important. If you'll die because you are ill-prepared and don't have what you need, then risking your life to get what you didn't before would be something you may need to risk dying trying to find.

Gather

Hopefully you will have your supplies already ready and ample food storage to start off and survive while hell rages outside your door. But we cannot live forever with a temporary food supply. We are always eating, and a food supply will never last forever so we need to constantly be getting more. As soon as it is safe, start hoarding more essentials. Food storage is supposed to give you something to get you started and be there when you can't find what you are looking for. It is not supposed to be a permanent source of calories. If you could gather perishable products like you do now when you go to the super market and can keep your food storage full, you'll be living the life long lusted by collapsed societies. Variety is the spice of life. Ask any soldier, eating MREs are great for a few days, but they'll soon lose their appeal. Dried powdered meat just doesn't compare to a fresh steak.

Here are a few things you can do to get food:

- Hunt
    - The food with the most calories is animal flesh. The freshest food is still alive. But eating it while it is still living isn't the most fun (or healthiest) thing to do. Hunting takes care of that problem. You can hunt animals as small as mice to as big as elephants.

- Fish
    - Especially useful way of getting food when around a well-stocked water source. Be cautious about fishing in places where dead fish can be seen. Never eat a fish you find floating in the water.

- Trap
    - An easier way of getting meat without actually being there. This can also extend what you can eat. Some animals are really difficult to hunt, but bait and a snare can capture what you can't shoot.

- Gather
    - We can't live off of wild meat alone. Vegetables, fruits, and grains are all essential and need to be in our food supply. Gather and store these foods, because they aren't always in season. The wild, a garden, or an abandoned house may all yield food that can keep you healthy and alive.

- Grow
    - It requires less work than walking and you get more when you grow your own food. This can be not only planting gardens but also animal pens.

Store

We can't eat a whole cow in a day but wasting a hundred plus pounds of beef because of our limited stomach size isn't the greatest idea either. Fruits are a great source of vitamins and all we have to do is pick them off the tree. How are we going to get our vitamin C in the winter when the only thing on the trees is snow? The only way to have a healthy and balanced supply of healthy and balanced food is to have proper ways of storing meals for later.

Death and disease are likely to occur even if people can still fill their bellies. Having a variety of storable foods will help keep the essential vitamins in your diet that are necessary to keep your immune system strong.

Some ways to prepare food to last longer include: drying, brining, canning, cooking, smoking, etc. Fire, salt, or even a hot car with a cracked window can help to stop food from spoiling. Once the vitals are prepared, you need a good place to keep them. Besides a freezer, a cool dry place is the best place to store your prepared goods.

Basements are great, but any good hole in the ground would work.

Secure what you store

Having a pile of food shining like a lighthouse on a hill is not going to remain in your possession for long. An open door to what you store is going to leave you empty-handed and everyone else with something you worked so hard to get. Have ways to hide/protect your supplies. (See also Security Devices for some ideas to secure your stash.)

Here are some things you can do:

- Walls, doors and locks. Have a building to put it in. The simplest of structures can be a great first step to deter would-be thieves (not to mention the elements). Anything with four walls and a roof can hide valuables and stop them from being taken.
- Trip wire, motion detectors, advanced warning devices, anything to give you a heads up when someone is approaching. Be ready to defend it if the alarms go off.

Fuel Alternatives

Even though most do not have the expertise or equipment to drill into the earth to get flammable fuels, there are alternative methods of acquiring fuel. These methods aren't commonly used in production because they cost more than they produce, but if we are in a survival situation, these methods can be a life saver.

Fuel source	Alternative source
Ethanol (gasoline)	Yeast, sugar, and water fermented and distilled.
Diesel	Bio fuel: cooked and filtered fat
Propane	Wood gas: Gas taken from wood in a metal container put in a fire. Hydrolysis: Using electricity to separate water into oxygen and hydrogen. By connecting a tube above the positive terminal, you can collect the very flammable hydrogen gas.
Electricity	Generator/alternator powered by wind, water or muscle. Solar power. Converting sunlight into electricity Stored in batteries (car batteries work great for mass storage)
Coal	Wood burns nearly as good, rolled newspaper burns like wood.

Dealing with Visitors

No matter what plan you feel is best for you, there are others who feel and will follow the same solution. Paths are bound to be crossed. But not everyone you meet will be out to get what you have. Some people may just be passing by; others may be looking for help. Some can become a lifesaving ally while others a life-threatening crook.

Carnage with confrontation kills. The best way to stay alive is to avoid altercations. Don't get leered into the bravo of fighting. People die there; don't be among the bodies.

One of the serious dangers with visitors is the diseases they carry. I'm not just talking about some apocalyptic plague. Diseases are passed from person to person. Any time we make contact we share germs. Without readily available medicine, who knows what diseases may become fatal? Observe visitors and pick up on the signs of sickness. Be cautious with contact and wash your hands frequently.

How you deal with visitors can save or sacrifice your life. Here are your basic options:

Confront

If you feel it is safe or if you have a way of ensuring your safety, go ahead and see what the visitor wants. What you do with their requests is completely up to you.

There are of course dangers to this plan. You are giving away your position. If you can live in this place than you obviously have supplies to do so. A few people may not be a threat, but they can return with more who can be. A confrontation may seem safe, but it may be a trap. Use your brain before you extend your hand of friendship.

Hide

Observe without being observed. You don't always need to ask to discover what someone's intentions are. Watching can give you plenty of answers.

If you have no interest in moving out because of a knock at the door, then don't answer. The problem is that not all people are going to leave because of an unflinching door. Hiding may work for someone just passing by, but it may be impossible to hide all signs of life and anyone seeing life may start hunting. If you are good at hiding than you may need to be patient as you watch your stuff ransacked.

Run away

"He that fights and runs away,

May turn and fight another day;

But he that is in battle slain,

Will never rise to fight again."

–Tacitus

If you are facing an enemy vicious and powerful, the best solution may be to get out of there quickly. You may have to leave some supplies for the wolves to take instead of you, but you started over at doomsday, you can do it again.

Running away exposes you. It's hard to hide when you are on the move. Starting over after doomsday can be fatal; no matter how many times we do it, but sometimes that is the risk we take to survive.

"But if he only runs at danger's sight,

He will never ever learn to fight.

And when a fight corners him

He will not have the chance to win."

Running is a great skill, but it isn't an option every time. Even if you are in the habit of running stay prepared just in case a corner corners you.

When Forced to Leave Your Home

We hope to never need to, but there are situations that can make your own homes an unsafe place to stay. As much as we would like to pack up everything we own to take with us when we flee, time or transportation take away that option. Even when not home we would like those things protected. Danger constantly comes and goes, and it would be nice to have an un-invaded place to come home to if the dust settles.

Here's how to protect your home if you have to leave it for a potentially long time and you have time to prepare:

- Board windows -- boarding both sides is even stronger.
- Board all doors except for one. Board the front door and leave a less obvious door as the only possible entrance.
- Install extra locks and lock all locks on the doors.
- For the unboarded entrance possibly install a drop-down bar, which can be lowered into place from the outside.

- Hide precious items in a secured hidden location, possibly a secret safe.
- Turn off gas, water, and electricity.
- Possible dissuasion techniques (trip wire, noise alarms, etc.) to scare away any intruders. Like traps in an Egyptian tomb to keep the treasures safe. Someone might gain entrance to the inside but with the house trapped they may call off a search.

Different Preparedness Plans

Just as there are different weapons and equipment that work best in different survival situations, there are also different survival plans. When it is time to bug out (or in) there are various safe places to go and plans to get there safely. We all have different preferences on where we want to live and how we like to travel. Have a preference for a plan that fits most to your talents, recourses, and needs.

Planning isn't like having a shopping list of things to buy when you need groceries. Supplies need to be purchased now if you want your plan to succeed in the future. This isn't only about supplies. Practicing the plan now is as essential as having the inventory.

Hopefully the plan you choose will suit your current surroundings. If you plan to take to the seas, then living a thousand miles inland isn't the best way to prepare. If you want to live in the wild, residing in the crowded center of a large city will make it hard to get there. You don't have to live in your survival setting but live close to where you hope to carry on.

Plans can change. A bunker may be a great safe place initially, but as supplies run out, the plan might need to be modified or even abandoned. Other times you may not be able to get to your safe haven and may need to find an alternative until you can. Prepare for multiple situations.

Get stocked, get practicing, and get close and familiar with your survival settings.

The Rural Plan

If the decision has been made to stay in a large rural area (possibly with only your immediate family), lock up tight. Your house may need to be turned into a fortress to fend off foraging foes.

More than any other plan, the rural plan puts you at most risk for disease. Being around other people in people's places puts you in the crosshairs of human diseases. Always practice good sanitation.

Transportation

Unlike other plans the rural plan is going give you better access to gasoline. Even with gas stations sucked dry there will be thousands of abandoned vehicles filled with the liquid gold. But as fuel dissipates, so will your ability to travel. Get off or lesson your dependence to gas. Use it only when you absolutely need to and have a sufficient way to store it.

Horses

- Because of feeding resources a horse may be a difficult form of transportation in a rural area. You won't be able find many horses anyways. If you do, it might make better food.

Car

- Because of the noise, size, and gas consumption this should not be frequently used in the rural plan. Roads may be blocked or barricaded, with your car adding to the pile. It is a great (and possibly only) way of transporting your family, but this is not recommended for a daily commute. Gas would cost an arm or a leg or it may literally cost you your life to obtain it after it is not being produced. Don't take the risk too often of using it.

Bicycle.

- Simple, silent, descent speed. This is not a bad self-powered vehicle to have. Great for scouting, but you can't carry the most gear with it.

Electric vehicle

- Combustible fuels may be hard to feed, but electric vehicles can feed off of anything. Solar, wind, water, even manpower can generate electricity to power an electric car. Careful with roadblocks. Because these vehicles are the size of a regular car, they are not the most maneuverable.

Motorcycle

- Uses very little fuel and can maneuver like a fast man on foot. One of the most efficient gas drinkers ever made. However, motorcycles are much louder than any car and the sound can attract unwanted pursuers.

On Foot

- Your quietest, most maneuverable form of transportation that will always be ready at a moment's notice. It also costs the least to use. Moving around on foot is going to be one of your most reliable and used ways to get around. Be ready for a lot of walking and sprinting when needed.

Shelter

There isn't any better shelter than your own home. But just because you are living at home, it doesn't mean you are still in a nice neighborhood. The best places have the greatest risks for invading marauders you once called friends. Lock up your house tight. This is more than locking your doors to prevent a bugging burglar. You need to ready your home to stop a complete home invasion.

We live in houses made of wood and dry wall. We don't live in stone castles and fortresses. As much as we build and block, our homes will never be able to withstand a large force. Our homes need to be able to keep us hidden as well as keep us safe. Your second-best strategy is to make it appear like you are not home. Sometimes hiding the fact that you are living there will dissuade thieves more than building strong towers with flood light security to tell everyone you have something that might be worth gathering an army to steal.

If you are going to have lights on at night, make sure to keep your windows completely covered. Seeing light can be a dead giveaway that the house is occupied. Before you go outside make sure you take the time to look around to make sure no one is watching.

Food and Water

This may be the most difficult part of urban survival. Ranches and woods aren't around to feed us. City streams and drains may long be contaminated and unsafe to dip a toe in, let alone drink. Your only food supplies may be in someone else's home. In an urban environment home invasion may be common. Empty or abandoned homes may be open game, but how will you know until you get in there? There is always a risk of going into someone's home. But starving can also kill you.

Before D-day occurs build up descent food storage, at least a year. If you can add to that with reusable resources, you will be able to survive longer. Mini or window gardens, potted plants, or herb farms all can continually supplement your food supply. Don't be afraid to dig up a lawn to plant something more edible.

Water is a whole other issue. You can store a year's supply of food in a closet, but a year's supply of water would flood the house. In a survival situation it is recommended to store one gallon per person per day. For one person for one year that is six 55-gallon drums; each one standing nearly five feet tall. An entire bedroom would be needed if you wanted to store enough water for a small family of three.

If you got the barrels and the space to store a room full of water, awesome! (A covered swimming pool might work for this cause) If you don't have the room (even if you do), then you are going to have to find a way to replenish your constantly diminishing water supply. Most cities were originally built around rivers and streams. These may still exist in a rural area but have been tunneled underground. Lifting manholes might mean a discovery of a drinkable dip. If you find clear water, it doesn't mean you can put a straw in and immediately hydrate. But after properly treating it, it can become drinkable.

Chances are obviously higher that you will find water not ready to drink than you will to find perfectly filtered and treated water. So you'll need to have a way to filter and treat rainwater, pond water, or whatever you can find. Charcoal and sand are some of the best materials easily be made or found that can filter water.

Boiling is the safest and most efficient way to make the water drinkable after it has been filtered.

Recommended kits

- Contamination kit
- Command Post (if in an apartment or house)
- Self-sustained sanctuary (if you have the space i.e. compound, factory, acreage, etc.)
- Warzone kit
- Security devices
- Security weapons

The Dangers

It is harder to hide in a rural area. Looters are likely to go from house to house looking for goods to add to their collection. You may be able to dissuade small groups, but what about large? Once they know you are there and obviously protecting something, they may mass a larger group. Unless you have a massive impenetrable security force, the best solution after an initial confrontation with intruders is to move away.

The more time in a city the harder it will be to find resources. A city dwelling may be a nice base, but you are going to have to travel further and further to get supplies. Each time you get supplies you put yourself in danger.

The Wild Plan

Another solution is deep in the mountains or forests; farther than most city-dwelling hunters would travel. Living in a place farther than a day's hike should be sufficient. This is not a day's drive up a mountain, but over a day's walk from a small trail. Mother Nature takes care of those who learn to come under her wing. It is isolated from the worries of the rural world. The wild could become your Garden of Eden if you prepare right.

You may need to raid to get supplies not found in the forest. But don't make a habit of it. Your goal is to get off the grid, not come crawling back after every problem you face.

Transportation

Off-roading vehicles may have some use, but where are you going to get refined gasoline in the middle of nowhere? These kinds of vehicles won't last long under a canopy. They are also loud, and the noise can summon unwanted guests; not to mention they leave large clear tracks for any enemy to follow.

Mountain bikes may be a viable option. But keep in mind that the mountain is rough even on bikes designed for it. Bikes are not maintenance free, so have the gear to keep your bikes functioning.

Horses are an excellent option. They are quiet and can cover nearly any terrain. They can carry us and heavy loads. They can feed off the land in the meadows God made for them. But we do need the gear to keep them healthy.

Your most likely used type of transportation is walking, so have some good boots and legs to match.

Shelter

Living outside exposes you to the elements, so make sure you have something to counter what may come. Build or find an insulated shelter. A cave may be a good option as this may be hidden better than a cabin in the woods.

In most cases you are going to end up building your own shelter. Most prebuilt cabins are too close to civilization and have large roads that can lead a looter straight to it.

When first in your area of residence, you may need a temporary structure to sleep in but work on making a more comfortable one that is better suited for all the seasons; especially the coldest one.

Having a roof over your head isn't going to keep you warm, so make sure you have a shelter with something to heat it. This is most likely going to be a wood burning fire. Gathering firewood is going to be a daily ritual. If you don't decide to gather wood until you are freezing to death, then you are already dead.

Food and water

The forest may be a near endless source of food, but there may be days (or winters) when food may be hard to find. Keep ample food storage. There may be fruits in the forest and vegetable in a garden, but neither are producing in the winter.

Become familiar with the plants and animals of your chosen environment. Just because a berry bush is close by doesn't mean it is edible. Having this knowledge of what to eat and what to avoid may definitely save your life. Water is always needed and can be found easily in a forest. If you find a good stream at the source you can have clean water year-round.

It doesn't have to be all about hunting and gathering. Even in the wild you can grow fruit trees and bushes, vegetable gardens and animals. Rabbits, chicken, cows, and sheep can all roam around your wild dwelling. Having pens and pastures can give you meat, milk, and eggs without you wandering the woods to find it.

Recommended Kits

- Self-sustained sanctuary
- Hunting kit
- Security devices

The Dangers

One of the biggest dangers in living in the wild is forest fires. Not only is it an all-destructive force that kills any person it catches, but it also destroys food sources, both plant and animal, dries up or contaminates water sources, and eliminates any shelter or concealment. It turns a lush landscape into a barren desert. Be careful with your own use of fire. Not just to prevent forest fires, but smoke from a fire can be seen from a long way away.

Another danger is wild animals. We may be able avoid harmful humans, but the farther from people we get, the more animals we are around. They are big and brutal or painful and poisonous. With the city population fleeing into the wild the wild creatures will have more encounters with man than their ancestors. The fear of man may go away. Instead of every man out in the wild carrying a gun, scavengers will be out in bear country with food in their hands and on their bones. After successful savage attacks the wild killers will lose their fear of man and may develop a taste for them.

We can't know everything and sometimes we are stuck in a situation we don't know how to handle, or physically can't. An example of this is an injury that would generally require surgery. Most people generally don't know how to perform an emergency surgery. Those who know may not have access to the required equipment in the middle of the forest. Even those who do won't be able to perform it on themselves. It's survival of the fittest. Lose that you may lose your life.

The biggest killer in a forest is the winter. Food becomes scarce. Animals are hibernating, hiding to conserve heat, or fled south. Plants aren't producing edibles eats. Even frost could bite you to death right outside the door. In order to survive not only do you have to have gathered most if not all your food, but fuel as well. Wood is easily gathered in the woods, and it would be best gathered when you don't have to dig through snow to find the wet wood. If you don't have enough food and fuel for feed and fire your efforts and life fall frozen.

The Ocean plan

When disaster strikes, those with a ship may take to the waters. It's not a bad idea. Oceans have plenty of food (and water if you got the equipment) that could keep you alive for a lifetime. Since ships are generally prepackaged with enough equipment to survive months at sea, planning and preparing to escape to the waters is as easy as planning for a trip.

Escaping to sea doesn't mean you can't ever come back to land, but the longer you can stay afloat the safer you stay. Ports are likely to be loaded with pirates, so it is recommended to stay away from them.

Escaping to the ocean can keep you safe from tsunamis (they only turn into waves close to shore, earthquakes (water ain't earth), and most of the other apocalyptic circumstances. If you have the gear and knowledge sea survival can be an excellent plan.

Transportation and Shelter

You should obviously have a boat that can shelter you, but possibly a smaller vessel to go to beach, or use in case of the main boat capsizing.

Having an alternative form to transport the boat is also recommended. If you have an outboard motor, possibly a backup sail or oars to move the boat in case the primary source fails.

Your boat will also be your shelter. Make sure it gives you shade from the sun, a shield from the rain, and dry from the sea.

Food and water

Water sources are full of fish. Use bait (less then humanly edible food i.e. fish guts) on fish lines or throw it out of the boat and shoot and pull in what comes to eat it.

Water is all around and having a system to filter and treat it will take care of any thirst. Have a backup available. If your main filter breaks without a backup, the ocean will turn into a barren desert.

The Dangers

You can escape on the ocean but there is no hiding. There is no way to camouflage a boat and no obstruction to hide behind or under. Unless you own a submarine your only option on a boat is too always run on the water.

A boat can be seen for miles around (from plane or boat), and not everyone who is looking is friendly. Just like on land, looters can roam the seven seas looking for supplies. If your boat is not faster, you are in for a fire fight that is very likely to damage, if not sink, your ship.

You may be able to avoid a tsunami but Mother Nature's deadliest force can still ride the seas. Storms are intensified on the ocean. Hurricanes can become a hundred-mile death trap.

Land-based resources are very limited on the water with fuel one of the biggest problems. The fastest way to travel by boat is by engine, but how are you going to fill a tank when the fuel tanks?

Recommended Kits

- Family survival kit
- Ocean Kit
- Urban Assault Kit
  - (If you plan to come to city ports for gear)

The Nomad Plan

With this plan you are on the move; going from location to location using the supplies around you until they are exhausted. Then pack up and finding another place. This may be temporary as you are traveling to a certain place to call paradise. You may need to use this plan if you are traveling across country.

This plan may also function using a plane for travel. Be cautious with where you touch down. Airports may hide those waiting for supplies to land. If you can scout from the skies do so.

Transportation

It is recommended that you use a light sports utility vehicle (SUV). This will give you off-road capability, could potentially hold up to eight passengers, and allow you to tow things if needed. The seats can even be folded down and an inflatable mattress put in to provide a safe mobile shelter to sleep in.

Attaching a grill guard to the front will allow you to use the vehicle to push obstructions out of the way without damaging the vehicle. Roads are likely to be overloaded with obstacles. If you can push a barricading car out of your way instead of risking a detour you can increase your chances of surviving.

For scouting new areas, it may be recommended to have another smaller vehicle instead of using a gas-hungry heifer. A motorcycle may be an option but can be loud, a bicycle may work better. Of course sometimes just using your feet may be the easiest way to get around when looking around. Always keep at least half a tank's worth of gas in portable gas cans in your vehicle and keep all tanks full as frequently as possible.

Shelter

You generally aren't going to be staying in a place long enough to build a shelter. What is the point of spending time and resources to build a home you may soon abandon? For the most part, shelter is whatever you may find. You may be living in an amazing, abandoned mansion one week and camping in your car the next. Wherever you decide to live keep your car loaded in case you need to escape in a hurry. Remember, it's not your home you're living in, and the previous residence may return.

Food and Water

Food is what you find. You may find full cupboards in an abandoned apartment or fresh game in a forest. It all depends on where you are passing. This isn't only about living off of the land. Keep a few weeks of food and possibly water in your vehicle and keep it fully stocked as often as you can.

Recommended Kits

- Mobile command post (if you have a trailer)
- Family survival kit (if you only have a car)
- Hunting kit
  - When staying away from the city this kit helps you to acquire food.
- City assault kit
  - This kit was designed to aid you in getting resources in an urban environment while helping to reduce the risk of conflict. Perfect for a wanderer looking for supplies.

The Dangers

The nomadic plan puts you in the most contact with people you are unfamiliar with. You may encounter people on the road and any place you stop. People won't know you either. The recipe for mistrust can easily bake into violence. Just as you want supplies, you have supplies other people also want. Some people don't want to talk. They may just shoot first and then take everything, starting with your life. Always use caution when meeting strangers in a desperate and dangerous world.

The Group Plan

This plan can be combined with any of the other aforementioned plans. The further away from large cities the better. A small group of families, a neighborhood, or a small town (less than a thousand-person population) can band together and provide enough food and protection for the inhabitants. This may be a viable solution. Whatever the group, there should be different responsibilities divided up.

These responsibilities could include:

Division	Purpose
Conflict resolution	Internal and external. Mediators that help to resolve conflict within the group. Also deal with negotiation and bartering with other groups. Different than security because it is less hostile and doesn't put too much power into those with weapons.
Security detail	Protection and possibly invasion. Includes separate night watch assignments, and scouting unit. Security devices, warzone, and city assault kit.
Medical	Complete medical kits, first aid, body removal, quarantine
Food	Finding and distribution. Hunting and scouting unit. Cooking and water prep. Hunting, gathering, gardening, and preservation of food.
Child keeping	Protects, teaches, plays with the children to keep them calm. Supervises and quiets (when hiding). Keeps them safe from traumatic experiences.
Maintenance	Fixes and maintains equipment. Cars, houses, etc. Has tools for the trade.
Fuel	Collecting, storing, creating, distributing fuel; be it solid (wood, coal), liquid (gasoline, oil), gas (propane, wood gas), or electrical (solar, battery, dynamo). Possible scout unit to retrieve potential supplies. Rents out full batteries and charging old ones.

Recommended Kits

Each family should have their own supplies consisting of the Command Post kit.

See "convey and community" in the survival kits section for an inventory of equipment each division should have.

The Dangers

It's hard to know who to trust. If you have a resource someone else feels they need, all friendship goes out the window. You may feel like you are getting an unfair share of community wealth.

Because there is a chain of authority, someone could get power hungry and initiate a martial law to control those under him. Your free society can quickly turn into a labor camp.

Big groups can potentially be big targets for even bigger groups. It is harder to hide a mass of people and there is always going to be a bigger hungry fish out looking for profitable pickings. There is a safety in numbers, but it can also create a large target for larger forces.

If you could live on a cloud, would it matter what happens below it? Earthquakes, tsunamis, pandemics, drugs; none will affect you if you live above it all. Wouldn't the safest place be in a plane or balloon that never needs to land? What about living in a space station?

It does sound safe, but cutting yourself off from the earth presents too many problems. All your resources are down there. Fuel, food, water, etc. You may have a supply in the sky, but what do you do when that runs out. Not even space stations are self-sustained sanctuaries. They depend on ground control and supplies being brought up.

Traveling in the skies may be the safest after doomsday. There is almost no chance of being followed unnoticed or having pirates attack from the sky. No worries about roads that are blocked, and no one can stop you. Military planes could shoot down passenger planes, but that would be pointless. If someone wants your supplies, shooting you down and searching through burnt out wreckage won't give them much of anything. Flying may be safe, but living in the sky isn't really practical.

Boats don't always have to park at a port when coming to land, but most airplanes need a long clear runway. Most planes but not all. Small bush planes don't need as large of an area to land, and – depending on the condition of land – may not even need a runway. Pontoon planes only need water.

If you are trying to isolate yourself from a chaotic society, a small plane is a great way to go and get gone. It can get you farther quicker and can go places other vehicles could never reach. It can take you to your island, bunker, cabin, or boat before anyone else can get there. A plane is not trackable from the ground, if you were found and forced to flee.

Planes can be seen from miles away, and they can be heard just as far if not farther. It is easy to hear a plane a see where it is landing. Before landing in your safe zone pass over a couple times to scout and make sure no one is nearby to greet you with a gun.

A plane will not be a common commuting contraption in a world with little fuel. It can get you to your planned place of survival, but may only have a few flights available, so don't wander with your head in the clouds.

I have not mentioned helicopters, because they are not as practical as a plane. They cannot travel the distance of their winged cousin, and they take incredible amounts of fuel to keep the propellers propelled.

GENERIC SURVIVAL KITS

Survival Basics:

Following is a list of the basics for survival. They have abbreviations that will be seen in the kits so you can know what basic essential the item is covering.

- Food (FR food reserve, or FA food acquisition): Provides means of getting nourishment and calories or is a means of preserving nourishing necessities.
  - Calories need to be taken in not only to survive but to do any kind of work. We can only last about 2 weeks without food.
  - Minimum of 1500 calories a day is recommended for an adult.

- Water (W): Helps to obtain and hold suitable drinking water or is suitable water source.
    - Besides air, water is our most important resource. We can only last a couple of days without water.
    - It is recommended to store one gallon of water per day for an adult.
- Shelter (SH): Provides protection from the elements.
    - The more we are affected by the weather, the more the chance of losing our health and possibly our life. The less we expose the better.
- Heat (H): Assists in the maintenance of proper body temperature.
    - Even with a shelter, during the cold nights and winters an extra heat source may be needed to live through the chill.

- Safety (SA): Protects or provides warning from hostiles.
  - When we have valuable resources, others may attempt to harm us and steal them. Also there are animals we need to protect ourselves from.
- Cleanliness (CL): Provides sanitation to fight disease.
  - If we lose our health, we lose everything else. Fighting disease is an important part of fighting for our lives.

- Mobility (M): Assists and aids in movement of both person and equipment.
  - Whether to find resources or to move locations we need help in traveling.
- Communication (CO): Acquiring or sending information.
  - News updates can be important in finding out the safety of an area, finding other survivors, and keeping organization.

- We are not always close to the members of our survival group but may still need to immediately communicate with them, especially to warn of danger they cannot see.

Mini Survival Kit (fits in a daypack)

This kit is entirely pre-packed with bare essentials that aid in requiring necessities. It can be grabbed at the most urgent of emergencies (a great bug out bag). It can possibly be left in a car when no time to pack is available. It contains tools to make all survival basics. This mini kit may have the largest inventory, but all the items are small to fit in a small sack.

PERSONAL ITEMS	
Item	**Description and Purpose**
Hiking Boots	(H) Waterproof preferably
Wool Socks	(H) Wool is the only material that can keep you warm even when wet.
shirt	(H) Preferably thick Polyester that dries quickly if wet to reduce the risk of hypothermia
Pants	(H) Good, rugged pair that can stand up to being worn around.
Jacket	(H) Wind breaker, water resistant

Item	Description and Purpose
Daypack	(M) Smaller than a backpack. Fanny pack sized.
Water Filter	(W) Something small that doesn't take up much space. Straw and filter.
Fire Starting kit	(H) Little bit of tinder and something to light it. Because of repeating use, flint and steel, fire piston, or magnesium strip is recommended. None of these are affected by water submersion.
Survival Knife	(SA, FA) Heavy duty sheath knife that can carry fire starting kit, fish line, etc.
Poncho	(SH) Keeps you dry when raining. Foldable and portable, possibly camouflage to help you hide if needed.
Garbage Sacks	(SH) Can be used as anything that needs to be waterproofed, rain/ground tarp, hanging bag, poncho, etc.
Emergency Blanket	(H) Very portable and can keep you warm. Combined with poncho can keep you warm, dry and hidden. Reflective, can also be used to signal for help.
Radio	(CO) Small possibly solar or crank powered. Radios can't be tracked but can give you a method of receiving information.
Signal Mirror	(CO, H) The best way to signal any help in sight without drawing attention to those you don't want to.

	Foldable Shovel	(SH) Entrenching tool can be used to build shelters. With a serrated edge you can use it as a saw, ax, or weapon.
	Binoculars	(SA) When traveling, use these often to make sure no one is watching you.
	Head lamp	(SA) Because of easy visibility at night and limited battery life, use a night light with caution.
	Mini Solar charger	(SA) Helps to charge light, battery, radio, cell phone, or any other small appliance. Possibly part of a solar radio.
	Mini First Aid Kit	(CL) Injury treatment.
	Fishing stuff	(FA) Fishhooks, line and reusable lures. Possibly in survival knife.
	Rope and wire	(SH, FA, SA) can help tie a lean to, make a snare, make a trip wire, etc.
	Auto reel	(FA) Great for fishing without waiting the whole day by the water. Many other uses as well.
	Bear Bells	(SA) Get a couple of these. Helps to keep the bears away. Can be attached to the auto reel or trip line to alert you to something moving the string.
	Sling	(SA, F) small simple weapon that can use rocks for ammo.

Survival Pack (fits in a backpack)

At least partially packed. All necessary essentials included. This pack can be put together with only a moment of preparation. When needs require to carry only the essentials. Allows for easier access to survival basics. This pack alone also provides a great hunting pack. Can be carried on foot or by some other smaller means of transportation (i.e. horse, bike, etc.) which may be added to this kit.

Item	Description and Purpose
backpack	(M) Preferably with a quiver attached so that it holds both gear and arrows
Mini Survival Kit	All the items in the previous kit. This bag can be pulled from this survival pack if gear needs to be quickly discarded.
Take down bow and Arrows	(FA, SA) Good for hunting big and small game, and can also be used to fish. Effective for quick shooting in a barricaded situation. Gives you some protection at a distance. Can be taken apart and put in the backpack.
Water tablets	(W) A better way of purifying water.
Energy bars	(FR) For times you can't find food, this could give you the energy to continue.
Canteen	(W) Holds water for travel.
Multi-function pocketknives	(SA) Gives multiple tools for many different situations. Choose your favorite.

Folding Saw	(SH) A more efficient way of cutting lumber for snares, shelters, etc.	
Mini first aid kit	(CL) Helps more injuries and lasts longer than the smaller kit.	
Hearing device	(SA) Just like how binoculars can help your vision, get something to enhance your hearing. It will make it more difficult for someone to sneak up on you.	
Solar Powered lantern	(SA) A little more light to brighten your shelter.	
Cell phone or 2-way radio	(CO) Cell phone if communication is still intact. A satellite phone may be better. Because these can still be tracked keep off until ready to use.	
Walking stick	(SA, M) Not just a stick you find in the woods. Get something that has multiple purposes, i.e. a knife in the handle, a compass, etc.	
PERSONAL ITEMS		
Boonie hat	(SH) Maximize shade around the head with least visual obstruction.	
Shades	(SA) Polarized, durable helps you too see clearer in bright light.	
Shorts	(M) Something comfortable but still needs pockets.	

Basic Survival Kit (fits in a duffle bag).

Basic aids for essentials. When there is a form of transportation not your own, so you don't have to carry it (i.e. car, canoe, commuting vehicle, etc.).

Item	Description and Purpose
Duffle Bag	(M) Possibly waterproof.
Survival Pack	All the items in the previous kit. The pack can be pulled from this survival kit if gear needs to be quickly discarded.
Drip Filter	(W) Filters larger amount of water.
Universal Tools	(SA, M) Crescent wrench, pliers, screwdrivers, and sockets.
Fire Blanket	(SH) protection against a fire, can put out a fire quickly, or cover yourself in a fire.
Solar Charger	(SA) Larger, can connect to anything to charge, from cars to computers.
Hatchet	(SH) Goes through trees quicker than a saw.
Portable First Aid Kit	(CL) See first aid kits.
Trap Kit	(FA) Has the basics for trap making.
Bivy Sack	(SH, H) A small portable shelter. Basically a waterproof sleeping bag.
Multivitamins	(FR) Ensures proper nutrition even when it becomes hard to find the food for a balanced and healthy diet.
Machete	(SH, SA) Many uses outside of the jungle.
Pepper Spray	(SA) Small compact and more likely to disable and dissuade an attacker (person or animal) than even a bullet.

PERSONAL ITEMS	
Coat	(H) Something for the winter.
Thermals	(H) Base layer to keep you warm.
Outer layer pants	(H) Windproof water resistant.
Gloves	(H) Winter kind.

Basic Individual Kit (fits in a backpack).

Equipment specific to the person. Pack set aside with some stuff already prepacked*. Each member of the family grabs the pack and fills it with the other essentials. Not all prepacked because we are growing out of clothing and preferences change.

	Item	Description and Purpose
	Backpack*	(M) Like a school backpack. Fits all this gear.
	Coat	(H) Outer layer to provide the best protection from the elements.
	Blanket	(SH) A real blanket not only provides warmth but feels like home.
	Poncho*	(SH) Water and weather protection.
	7 pairs of socks	(H, C) Having a change of socks is one of the best ways to keep your feet clean and disease free.
	Sandals	(M) Quick breathing foot protection.
	5 sets of clothes	(H) Pack for different environments.
	Soap *	(C) Personal bar.
	2) Towels*	(C)Personal towels help them last longer.
	2) rags*	(C) Having your own pair keeps you cleaner and lasts longer.
	Portable pillow*	(SH) A soft sack to rest the head.
	Memories	(Psychology) Whether it's a journal or pictures. Small items.

Family Survival Kit (fits in a trunk).

Equipment is not yet bulky but essential for various different situations. For when you have your own form of transportation (car or cart). Family can survive for three days before resupplying. A kit for a family traveling on the run.

Item	Description and Purpose
Basic Survival Kit	All the items in the previous kit. The bag can be pulled from this survival pack if gear needs to be quickly discarded.
Individual Kits	All items included in previous kit for each member.
Car kit	All items included in the specialized kit.
First aid Kit	(C) See first aid kits.
Tent	(SH) Small enough to be portable, large enough to fit your family.
Sleeping bags	(H) One for each member. In compression bag to save space.
Water cooler	(W) One gallon per person per day.
Snowshoes	(M) Walk out and find essentials even when your car is snowed in.
Fire starter pack	(H) Little, compact, easily ignitable dry material.
IR water filter	(W) Simple way to disinfect water.
Axe	(SH) Large way to quickly cut entire trees for timber.
Dog (recommended not required)	(SA) Alert system with better eyes, ears, and nose. Also improves morale.

Snack bars and sandwiches	(FR) Two per person per day.
Gas can and siphon	(M) Two gal can. Always keep full and fresh.
Portable outhouse	(C) Sometimes you need to stop so you can go with no toilet.
Camo netting	(SA) large enough to conceal a car.

Mobile Command Post (fits in a trailer or truck bed).

Large but equipment is designed to be portable. A trailer or truck bed is required for transportation, but this is bare minimum for a set up at home. Can be locked at home and transported in shifts with a regular vehicle. Family can survive for three weeks without replenishing supplies. Can be a kit for extended travel.

Item	Description and Purpose
Family Survival Kit	All items included in specialized kit.
Psychology Kit	All items included in the specialized kit.
Weapons Repair Kits	(SA) Helps maintain your equipment so you can use it for longer.
50-gal Water Barrel	(W) For filtered and treated water. Don't mix with anything else.
Deep Cycle Battery	(SA) One of the best batteries to store electricity.
Solar Charger	(SA) 30-watt output minimum.
Camo clothes	(FA) Improves your chances of hunting success.
Trapping Kit	(FA) All equipment in specialized kit.
Tool set	(M) Basic sockets, wrenches, and a hammer fit snuggly in a toolbox.
Solar oven	(FA) Cooks food by the power of the sun.
3 weeks supply of food	(FR) Nonperishable preferably.

	Camping gear	(SH) Tents, sleeping bag, everything you would take on a trip
	Satellite phone	(CO) Suggested. Maintains communication.
	Log Roller	(H) Rolls paper so that they burn like wood. Augments your wood supply.
	Compound bow or Crossbow	(FA, SA) Offers greater distance for food hunting and security. At least two dozen arrows.
	Fishing Pole and Tackle	(FA) Provides a better means of catching fish than a string and hook.
	Portable Wood Pile	(H) A couple boxes full.
	10-gal gas can	(M) Extra gas for long rides or backup storage.
	Solar Shower	(CL) Uses the sun to heat water to be used to stay clean.
	Off-road Motorcycle	(M) Suggested if there's room. Great for scouting without using the large vehicle. Bicycle is an alternative.

Command Post (fits in a storage room)

Enough to sustain the family for a year. Can all be moved – in shifts – if needed. Family can survive a year without replenishing the supplies. Can be used in a shelter or bunker situation. Portions are for a family of four (2 adults, 2 kids)

	Item	Description and Purpose
	Mobile Command Post	All the items in the previous kits
	Food: 1 year	(FR)Dehydrated and MREs. Minimum 1500 calories per person per day.
	1200 gal of water 24) 50 gal barrels of water	(W) If you can, constantly replenish this supply. Even bunkers can collect rainwater. Need 100 gal/month just to drink.
	2) 100 lb. Propane tanks	(FA, H) for Heaters, light, and cooking.
	3-month supply of firewood	(FA, H) Since firewood can be easily gathered, this is a more reusable resource than propane.
	Rainwater retriever	(W) This collects clean water that is almost drinkable. A better source than a muddy contaminated stream.
	Toilet Paper: 1 year	(C) 122 roles.
	Soap: 1 year	(C) 17 bars.
	Razors: 1 year	(C) 12 pack.
	Shampoo: 1 year	(C)2 large bottles

.	Shaving Cream	(C) 2 - 4 cans.
	Toothbrush and paste	(C) 3 tubes, 2 brushes per person.
	Feminine hygiene products	(C) 12 boxes.
	Large pot	(W)To boil water.
	Diesel Generator	(SA)Used with the Diesel or biofuel.
	Deep cycle gel batteries	(SA) Stores energy for use when it cannot be generated.
	Stationary bike power converter	(SA)Reusable source of energy, man powered. Can be used when solar or wind power aren't available.
	Hand powered washer	(CL) for washing clothes.
	Propane outdoor cooker	(FA, W) To boil water and to cook.
	Propane Generator	(SA) Used with propane or wood gas.
	Sandbags	(SH) Protection and flood assurance.
	2x4s boards, and nails	(SH) Ideal for securing a home.
	smoker	(FA) a very effective and tasty way of preserving meat.
	dehydrator	(FA) an effective way of preserving most foods.
	Solar charger	(SA) 90 w charger is recommended.

Self-Sustained Sanctuary

Reusable/production resources. This is a permanent location with rarely a need to seek assistance from an outside source. Can be one home or a community with supplies divided between the households. The equipment would be difficult to transport and may need to be abandoned in case of an evacuation.

	Item	Description and Purpose
	Command post	All items included in above kit.
	Specialized kits	All items in every specialized kit.
	Horses	(M) Don't forget stables and space for them to move and live.
	Chickens and pen	(FA) A continued source of protein in both meat and eggs.
	Bee Hives	(FA, SA) to make honey, and helps in pollinating your plants.
	Garden	(FA) Seeds, soil, and tools for your green thumb.
	Perimeter security and warning system	(SA) (see Security Detail)
	House sizes solar panels	(SA) combined with others, can completely power a house on a sunny day. 200+watt charger(s)
	Automotive tools	(M) Fix, improve, and maintain a mode of transportation.
	Forge	(SA) Furnace, bellows, anvil, and hammer to manipulate metal.

	Welding Station	(SA) Welder and accessories.
	Wood working station	(SA) Multiple saws for the hand and table. Plug and hand powered.
	Well and water tower	(W) If you can dig a well, you'll never have to worry about water.
	freezer	(FR) If you have the power, might as well use a more efficient means of storing food.
	Windmill	(SA) Reusable source of electrical energy.

SPECIALIZED SURVIVAL KITS

Car kit

Stays in the car at all times.

Item	Description and Purpose
Tool bag	Keep your equipment in one easy to find place in the trunk.
Sun Shield	To provide shade for sleeping and possible sun signal.
Emergency blanket	Can fit in a glove box and pulled out keep you warm.
Multi wrench	Self-adjusting tool can work on any bolt.
Multi socket	Self-adjusting tool that can work on any bolt and reach places a regular wrench can't.
Tire iron	Collapsible for storage convenience.
Pocket knife	Can be used for self-defense, to cut the seatbelt, hoses, or to bash out a window to escape. Placed in reach of driver and passengers.
pliers	Strip wires, pull stuff.
screwdrivers	Both Phillips and flat.
Emergency light	Possibly one that can be solar powered or charged by your car.
Gas can	A small one is fine as you don't want to carry a huge full one after walking to a not-so-near gas station.
Slick platform	Helps to get vehicle out of snow, mud, sand, etc.

	Water	To drink or for the car.
	Jump starter	Can plug in devices, jump start battery, and inflate tires.
	Power inverter	Can convert your cigarette lighter into a regular outlet.
	Individual first aid	See first aid kits
	Fuses and checker	Many major motor malfunctions are fixed with a fuse.
	Check light	This helps you test electrical connections.
	Code reader	To find why the check engine light is on, easiest way to solve the mystery of why the car is having problems.
	Snow brush/scraper	Clears off snow and ice from the windows.
	Car Solar Charger	To charge small devices, car battery, and jump starter. Don't worry about using the vehicle's radio or lights if you got this and the sun to keep your battery from dying.
	Tire repair kit	Plugs leaky holes that lose air. Spares are good but a car works better with the actual tire.
	Electric heater	You can run your tank dry using the engine's heater in a blizzard. And then where would you be if you were able to get the vehicle out? With this you can use the solar charger to keep the battery fresh and use this to help keep you warm and still have gas to get away.

Trapping supplies

There is more than one way to acquire meat. Trapping allows you to be at multiple places at once hunting the animals. While your traps are set you could be relaxing at home or doing some other task. This is a list of supplies designed to trap food. This kit doesn't necessarily kill or injure the creature it traps.

	Item	Description and Purpose
	Polycord rope	Is small but very sturdy.
	Wire	Perfect for making snare.
	Snares	Premade snares made of thick wire.
	Canvas sheets	To cover the top of a pit trap.
	Net	Can be thrown, set, or dropped onto an animal to immobilize it.
	Wood hooks	Can be screwed into trees and wood to secure the rope.
	Auto Reel	Used for fishing or securing small snares.
	Bait	Specific for the animal you are trying to trap.
	Ground anchors	Screw in ground stake often used to hold pet chains. Used to secure snare to the ground.
	Bear bells	Attached to snares to alert you when something has been caught in the snare.
	Trap Blueprints	Drawings and schematics to provide instructions to create traps.
	Live trap	Cage with a trap door.

Natural Scents

Baiting is an easy way to hunt or trap. Instead of wasting energy trying to find food, have food find you. Meat provides the most calories, so sometimes it is an investment to sacrifice less caloric foods as bait so that you can invest it for more calories. Since you are not burning energy chasing prey, sacrificing a little food can turn into a significant trade off. The following is a list of common scents to attract common wild animals.

Most predators (especially bears)
- Uncooked rotten meat

Raccoon attractant
- Chicken Broth
- Mint
- Fish juice

Rabbit attractant

- Lettuce
- Cabbage
- Carrots

Squirrel attractant

- Fruits
- Nuts (Pecans are one of their favorites)

Deer Attractants

- Pure apple juice
- Acorns
- Vanilla extract
- Corn
- Peanut Butter
- Molasses
- Deer poop
- Deer urine
- Black Liquorish

Fish

- Fish guts, fish eggs
- Corn
- Insects

Natural human scent eliminators to cover your smelly tracks that may scare off a potential prey.

- Cedar
- Pure apple juice
- Baking soda and water

Hunting Kit

A kit designed especially for hunting all sizes of game. Equipment can be carried in a backpack so you can travel light on your feet. Make sure your camouflage equipment is appropriate for your environment.

Item	Description and Purpose
Survival pack	Includes bow and arrows. Mini pack doesn't have to be included.
Motion sensors	Put on game trails to tell you when an animal passes.
sled	Can be used to drag gear and game over the ground.
Blind	A portable and collapsible camouflage hiding place.
Umbrella	Camouflage that can strap to a tree. Combined with the blind this makes a great camo shelter.
Camo Poncho	Packed up nicely in a pack. Keeps you blended in even when it's raining.
Field dressing kit	Skinning knife, game shears, gloves.
Mosquito repellant	Especially close to water sources. Something that is scent free.
Blood tracker light	Highlights spilt blood to more easily follow blood trail to fresh killed meat.
Natural Scents	Applicable scent for whatever you are hunting.

	Game calls	Audible bait to attract and locate potential dinners.
	Knee pads	Crawling is a common way to stalk. These protect your knees.
	Boot covers	This quiets your feet when stalking.
	Binoculars	Something to help you see more details farther away.
	Hoist and gambrel	Used to dress and clean large animals.
	Camp stool	Foldable and portable seat to rest your rump above the dirt.
	Compass	When wandering in the woods you'll need a way to find your way out.
	Wind detector	Always stalk downwind. You need to know which way that is.
	PERSONAL ITEMS	
	Hiking Boots	Water and snake proof preferably.
	Wool Socks	Wool is the only material that can keep you warm even when wet.
	Camo vest	Keeps small gear accessible.
	Camo shirt	Long sleeve. Moister wicking.
	Camo windbreaker	A light jacket to keep the wind from chilling the body.
	Camo pants	Rugged pair that is burr resistant.
	Camo gloves	A light pair that keeps hands covered and warm.
	Camo hat	Helps hide hair and protect from the sun.
	Camo mask	Covers the face so that it too blends in.

Winter Additions

Used with the hunting kit when hunting in cold and snowy weather.

	Item	Description and Purpose
	Snowshoes	Keeps you traveling faster and above the snow.
	Winter Poncho	White. Doesn't necessarily have to be waterproof.
	Winter coat	Graded for the minimum temperature you travel in. Doesn't have to be camo if used with the poncho.
	Insulated pants	Doesn't have to be thick and bulky if you layer well.
	Hand warmer	Chemical is possibility, but a reusable butane one would be better.
	Hand muffs	Extra warmth for your hands.
	Winter gloves	White, snow proof, insulated.
	Boot cover	Adds another layer of insulation.
	Wool hat	Keeps head and ears warm.
	Neck gaiter	Keeps neck warm and can cover the face.
	Ankle gaiter	Keeps snow from falling between your pant leg and boots.
	Sunglasses	The white of the sun and snow can cause snow blindness. Shades protect the eyes.

Ocean Kit

This kit is stored in a boat and waiting for survival on the waves.

Item	Description and Purpose
Family survival kit	Almost everything in this kit can be applied to ocean life.
Harpoon gun	A weapon for underwater hunting.
Snorkel gear	Basic swimming aid can be used with a harpoon.
Air compressor	Refills the scuba tanks. Charged by solar panels.
Scuba gear	Aids in getting food deeper and longer under the waves.
Fishing pole and tackle	Basic means of providing protein without leaving the boat.
Fishing spear	A little more difficult in getting fish but still has a use.
Scuba knife	Rustproof and some even float.
Sea water filter	Reverse osmosis is the best for turning sea water into drinking water.
Solar panels	Another way of charging any electrical equipment.
Fishing arrows and reel	A small harpoon you can shoot from your bow.
Skin moisturizer	Being around water can dry the skin to bleeding. This prevents that.

Sun screen	There is no shade on the ocean. This provides some protection against sunburns.
Burn ointment	To treat sunburn.
PERSONAL ITEMS	
Wet suit	Insulated suit keeps heat in the body.
swimsuits	Clothes that dry quickly and are designed to get wet.
Survival suits	This may be more important in arctic temperature, but falling overboard at night could cause you to freeze to death no matter where the boat is bobbing.
Life vest	Be in the habit of wearing this.
Sunglasses	Sun reflects everywhere on the ocean; unprotected eyes can go blind. Get some good protective shades.
Wide brimmed hat.	Stops some sun from scalding the skin on your face.
Sandals and water shoes	Hoping on land often requires walking up shallow water. Not all beaches are full of soft sand.

Improves morale. More of a luxury but very important.

	Item	Description and Purpose
	Memories	Whether it's a journal or pictures, etc. Small sentimental items.
	Games	Deck of cards, board games, portable video games.
	Pet	There is a reason pets are used in therapy. They help people feel better.
	Small hobby	Musical instruments, writing equipment, sewing, etc. Whatever you're interested in.
	scriptures	Spiritual health is an important aspect of health.
	Kindle	Can store many books and an extremely large battery life. More durable than paper.
	Sports equipment	Frisbee, soccer ball, football. All don't require large extra equipment to play.

Convoy or community kits

A group of people banded together for survival: separate families or groups with each playing a specific part. Many of these divisions can overlap but have specific leadership which calls on help from members of the other groups. Each group has supplies of mobile command post plus a specialized kit (when applicable).

Division	Purpose
Conflict resolution	Internal or external. Negotiation and bartering. Different than security because less hostile and intimidating.
Security detail	Protection and possibly invasion. Includes separate night watch assignments and scouting unit. Security devices and city assault kit.
Medical	Complete medical kits, body removal, quarantine. (See First aid kits).
Food	Finding and distribution. Scout unit. Cooking and water prep. Hunting, gardening.
Child keeping	Protects, teaches, plays with the children to keep them calm. Keeps them safe from traumatic experiences. Psychology kit.
Maintenance	Fixes equipment. Tools.
Fuel	Collecting storing, creating, distributing fuel; be it wood, gas, or electricity. Possible scout unit. Checking out full batteries and charging old ones.

Conflict resolution

No Kit required.

Security Kit

See Combat/confrontation kits

Medical

See First aid kits

Food

	Item	Description and Purpose
	Propane stove	Foldable portable, can cook anything a kitchen stove can.
	Solar food dehydrator	Can be a car, or mesh screen you can hang.
	Portable fire pit	A shallow hole in the ground would work just fine too.
	Dutch oven(s)	Cook in coals or on stoves.
	Solar Oven	Reflects and concentrates solar energy to heat and cook food.
	Greenhouse	Grows plants while using less water. If heated can be year round.
	Bleach	Food sanitation and water purification.
	50 gal Barrels of water	Collective barrel. Rations may be divided.
	Portable water containers	Collapsible. Sending a scout party out retrieve water which is pooled into a collective barrel.
	Traps and snares	See specific kit.
	Fishing gear	In trapping and mobile command post kits.
	Hunting gear	See specific kit.

Child keeping

	Item	Description and Purpose
	Individual Chalk boards	Small reusable method to write.
	Text books	Various subjects for various ages.
	Reading books	Picture to chapter books for all different reading abilities.
	Board games	Can be played by two people and others for a large group.
	Recreational equipment	All different kinds of sports. Keep kids active.

Maintenance

	Item	Description and Purpose
	Arch welder	Repair and create strong metal machines and tools.
	Woodworking equipment	Saws and sanders for the table or the hand. Muscle or electrically powered.
	Auto repair tools	Enough to take off and put on any part of the car.
	Forge	For manipulating the shape and density of metal.
	Household tools	To repair everything from plumbing to roofing.

Fuel

	Item	Description and Purpose
	Solar charger	To charge small batteries.
	Solar Panels	To charge larger batteries.
	Metal tank with spout	Fill with wood and put in a fire. The gas that escapes can be stored and used as a vapor fuel.
	Generator	Uses gas to produce electricity
	Windmill	Uses wind to produce electricity
	Car Batteries	Stores said electricity. Deep cycle would work the best.
	Small batteries	All rechargeable: AAA, AA, C, D, 9v
	Gas tanks	Different ones for different types of gas.
	Newspaper roller	Rolls paper into log-like rolls that burn like wood.
	Bike dynamo	Uses human power to generate electricity.
	Fermenter/ distiller	For making ethanol which can be used in place of gasoline.
	Divided water tank with stainless steel leads	Used to turn water into combustible gas (hydrogen). When electricity is connected to the leads it separates the water.

COMBAT/CONFRONTATION KITS

Security devices

Starts with most basic, simple, and smallest to largest, complex, and advanced. Operator does not need to stand at watch to be alerted. Divided by a Deterrent (D), or an alert (A).

Item	Description
hedge	(D) Natural barrier can grow your own or use what is already around. (beehives work great too)
Trip wire	(D) Thin wire secured at ankle height
Bells	(A) Attached to wire, string, doors, etc., to rattle when someone comes in contact with a deterrent.
Flash trigger	(A, D) Attached to trip wire can be a fire cracker, flash grenade, etc. not only raise an alarm, but scare perpetrator away.
Dog	(A, D) With the heightened senses a dog can detect approachers we can't and bark to warn or to ward off.
Barbed wire	(D) Can replace trip wire, used to top fences or make a fence. Doesn't need to be deadly wire.
Glass pieces	(A, D) Makes noise when stepped on and can also cause pain on animal and bare feet.
Caltrop	(D) Always lands spike side up, can be

		used to slow down both people and cars.
	Chain	(D) Attached to door and frame.
	sensor chime	(A) Sounds an alarm when sensors are separated works on windows too.
	Door Stop alarm	(D, A) Stops the door from opening completely and also sounds an alarm. Used with chain to completely stop intruders and sound an alarm.
	Motion light	(A, D) Motion sensor that turns on the light when someone passes within range.
	Motion sensor	(A) Sends a signal to a receiver when someone passes within range.
	Boards and 2x4s	(D) To put in front of doors and windows to permanently secure the entrance. Also good for storm proofing.
	Motion camera	(A) Turns on and takes a picture of anything crossing its path.
	Driveway sensor	(A)Sends a signal to a receiver when a car passes over the sensor.
	IR camera	(A) Flash camera that uses IR for the light. Great for nighttime vision without being seen.
	Video Camera	(A) Records video footage.
	Monitor	(A) View what your cameras are seeing.
	Wireless transmitter	(A) Transmits information from a sensor or camera to a receiver.
	Fence	(D) Chain link can be set up quickly and secured with a chain. Deters without obstructing vision.
	Metal rolled	(D) In front of large windows and glass

	gate	doors to add to security.
	Brick Wall	(D) Very difficult to get through can be built to support people on top.

Security Weapons

Non-fatal weaponry, riot control, or attack dissuaders held in hand.

	Item	Description
	Smoke grenade	Obscure sniper vision and can be a signal.
	Taser baton.	Self-protection like a knife that doesn't require slashing and killing. Makes a loud cracking noise to dissuade an attacker. Held in opposite hand like a combat knife.
	Cattle prod	A Taser with a longer reach.
	Stun gun	A Taser that can be shot up to 20 feet away.
	Pepper Spray	A great deterrent and can be shot at some distance. Can stop multiple attackers and help disperse a mob.
	Pepper Pellets	Used in a paintball gun, provides the most range of any of the deterrents.
	Mini flame thrower	More for intimidation than actual combat use.
	Whip	Intimidating way to keep people at bay. Not affective in close quarters.
	Riot shield	Ballistic window keeps you safe from chemicals and objects.
	Tear gas grenade	Used in a crowd or a room to cause eye and throat irritation.
	Flash grenade	Disorientation with a psychological effect.

	nets	Can be thrown or placed to temporarily immobilize an individual.
	Handcuffs/zip ties	Detains individuals by immobilizing hand or feet.
	Night stick or club	Can injure but decreases chance of fatality. Best protection against any hand-to-hand attack.
	Bolas	A weapon used to entangle someone at a distance. Can swing to keep crowd at bay and can be used as a club.
	Fire extinguisher	Disorients and blinds attackers. Offers a quick smoke screen.

Urban Assault Kit

After doomsday you may need a silent way to possibly deal with people and their stocked structures. Practice until you are proficient before you try to use them for real. This kit comes in three types: Day assault (D) night (N), and both (B).

Item	Description
Grappling Hook	(B) One of the quickest portable ways to get up and over walls.
Pepper Spray	(B) A great deterrent and can be shot at some distance. Can stop multiple attackers to buy you time to get away.
Lock pick set	(B) Opens locks without a key. Takes some practice to master.
Periscope	(D)To see up and around buildings and walls. A great way of seeing without being seen. Some even magnify.
Night vision monocular	(N) See at night without a seeable light to be seen.
Pistol Crossbow	(B)Fast close-range defense. Crossbow held in main hand during close combat. Can be used with laser sight and flashlight.
Binoculars	(D) Long range binoculars or spotting scope. For scouting and spotting before you go into a dangerous situation.

	Tactical crossbow	(D) Make sure this crossbow fires arrows (24 inches or longer) not bolts. A tactical crossbow can repeatedly blow out the bullseye from over 100 yards with little noise! An excellent stealthy sniping weapon. Great for single targets, but because of the slow loading time, not recommended for multiple attacking targets.
	Compound Bow	(B) Medium distant silent shooting. With fast reloading this can be used on multiple targets. Accuracy comparable to a pistol.
	Smoke bomb	(D)Provides quick concealment and disorientation. Can also help signal from a distance. Disrupts sniper vision. Do not use it unless presence is already detected.
	2-way radios	(B) Possibly hands free, with a throat microphone for quiet communication.
	Combat knife	(B) Held in non-dominant hand during close combat. Leaves other hand free to grapple, for the crossbow, or pepper spray. Last line of defense hopefully used more to cut ropes than limbs.
	Side/ Cat quiver	(B) Securely holds and hides the arrows and gear. If you have a side quiver have a separate backpack for your gear and strap the side quiver to that.

PERSONAL ITEMS	
Kevlar arm guards	Provides some protection against sharp objects like knives and teeth.
Bullet proof vest	Protects the vitals.
Helmet	Head protection, the more it can stop the better.
Kevlar facemask	Keeps your identity secret and protects you from knives slashing.
Knee pads	Sneaking around requires a lot of crawling.
Boots	A good pair you can run in.
Goggles	Protects the eyes.
fingerless gloves	Allows you to use your dexterous fingers and still gives protection. Some include hardened knuckles to increase punch power.

Warzone Kit

If outside your door becomes dangerous to go through and a huge threat of being invaded exists, you may need this kit. For such a dangerous situation it is probably best to leave where you live, but that is not always a timely option. This kit is not a stealthy kit like the City Assault Kit, nor is it designed to be less than lethal like the Defense tools. This is the kit recommended for the not recommended firefight. These items are all available for civilian use. If you can get your hands on military grade weaponry, more power to you – literally (Don't illegally obtain weapons. Don't break the law while it still exists).

Item	Description and Purpose
Urban assault kit	Everything in this kit can help you before the shooting begins.
Pick Axe	Two handed use. For busting down doors.
Pistol	Close range self-defense.
Shotgun	Devastating close range attack. Shotgun ammo can vary from close range (pellets) to a little further (deer slugs).
Assault rifle (AR)	Versatile weapon for rapid fire at close and far range.
Night vision goggles	Wearable to leave hands free to hold your equipment.
Flash/stun grenade	Blinds and disorients those close by.
Ammo	Extra clips for guns. Carry hundreds of extra bullets in a clip on your person for your AR, and dozens for your pistol and shotgun.
Mini first aid kit	Can fit in a pocket and can treat a gunshot wound.

First Aid kits

If you want, you can go to the store and pick up the prepackaged kits. These kits listed below have that store recommendation plus more.

Mini Kit

	Item	Description and purpose
	Mini first aid pack	Small pocket-sized kit you can buy in stores 20-30 items.
	Bandana	Can be used from everything from a sling, tourniquet, bandage, etc.
	Pocket scissors	To cut tape.
	Athletic tape	Goes over bandages to secure them in place.
	bandages	Non sticky sterile cloth.
	Super glue	Great to seal up small wounds.
	Coagulant	Clots and stops major bleeding.

Emergency First aid kit

	Item	Description and purpose
	Mini first aid kit	All the items included in the above kit.
	Small first aid pack	Small kit you can buy in stores 30-50 items.
	Acetaminophen	(Aka Tylenol) gentle and works on every kind of pain.
	Sports drink packets	Mix with water. Provides calories and also helps someone with low blood sugar.
	Tick remover	The best way to get off a tick.
	Snake bite kit	Small but essential in case you get bit.
	Tums	For a tummy in turmoil.
	Neosporin	Disinfects wounds.
	Neoprene gloves	To keep the rescuer safe from infection.
	Pocket knife	Various uses in a rescue operation.
	Benadryl	Allergy treatment both the pill and the cream.
	Alcohol	Sterilize and sanitize, both of the injured, the injury, and the rescuer.
	Wraps	Secures any wound without sticking like tape.
	Emergency blanket	Helps with treating shock. And can keep you warm.

Basic First Aid Kit

	Item	Description and purpose
	Medium first aid pack	Medium kit you can buy in stores. 50-100 items
	Tylenol suppositories	The other end might be the best way in If you have children.
	Excedrin	Headache relief
	Cough suppressant	Keeps a cough quieter.
	Burn relief	Cooling cream to quench scorched skin,
	Ice packs	Instant packs are recommended because they are easier to store. If you have plenty of ice in any form, use that first.
	Fire blanket	Puts out a fire on someone or protects someone from a fire.
	Epi pen	Extreme and quick allergy relief for serious symptoms.
	Ibuprofen	Anti-inflammatory pain relief.

Complete medical kit

Used with basic first aid kits to help transport someone who is injured.

Stock	Item	Description and purpose
	Large first aid pack	Large kit you can buy in stores 100+ items.
	Crutches	Helps someone who can only use one leg to still get around.
	Neck brace	Keeps an injured neck stable to prevent further injury.
	Sling	Secures the arm, shoulder and collarbone.
	Splint	Something straight and sturdy to secure to a joint so it doesn't move.
	Ankle brace	A quick way to secure the ankle so that the person can keep moving.
	Stretcher	Transporting someone safely. Takes multiple people.
	Body Bag	Hope you never need it, but with death common after the end...

Contamination Kit

Protects the wearer, destroys the contaminant. All these items can be easily purchased if you can't find a working bio suit. An essential kit for a pandemic.

Item	Description and purpose
Face masks	Provides some protection from airborne pathogens.
Disposable gloves	A barrier for the hands.
goggles	Protects the eyes.
Disinfectant wipes	Wipes surfaces to kill any disease on it.
Iodine tablets	Treats radiation poisoning.
antibiotics	Creams and pills to fight infections.
bleach	Kills pathogens.
Hand sanitizer	Use frequently. Hands are the biggest spreaders of disease.
Radiation detector	It's not only viruses that contaminate areas. This provides some warning.
Plastic apron	Creates a barrier for the body.
Gasoline	Destroying by fire contaminated material. Best way to destroy pathogens.
shovel	Burying contaminated material.
Alcohol	Kills pathogens wherever it's poured. Safe to use on bodies.
Duct tape	Secures the plastic to help quarantine an area.
Plastic wrap	Creates a barrier to prevent the spread of a disease.
Plastic bags	Put contaminated material in.

It is better to be more prepared than under. If you have a survival kit sitting ready for disaster and you never need to grab it, then be grateful. Those who train in self-defense or carry a gun and never are put in a situation to use it, won't regret carrying or learning the life-saving technique.

But there is always the "What if." What if someone does try to mug or attack me? What if I get in an accident the one time, I don't protect myself and put on a seat belt? What if Armageddon happens tomorrow? We won't regret what preparations we have done until we fall short of being prepared.

I hope that doomsday will never happen. I wish my life can continue uninterrupted by a catastrophe of any kind. I wish my family would always be safe and happy. If the unknown, unlikely, and unpredictable are more likely to happen than I wish to be ready for what comes from it.

NOTES:

www.ingramcontent.com/pod-product-compliance
Lightning Source LLC
Chambersburg PA
CBHW050446290526
45786CB00006B/2187